Design: Judith Chant and Alison Lee
Recipe Photography: Peter Barry
Jacket and Illustration Artwork: Jane Winton, courtesy of
Bernard Thornton Artists, London
Editors: Jillian Stewart and Kate Cranshaw

CHARTWELL BOOKS
a division of Book Sales, Inc.
POST OFFICE BOX 7100
114 Northfield Avenue
Edison, NJ 08818-7100

CLB 4259
© 1995 CLB Publishing, Godalming, Surrey, U.K.
Printed and bound in Singapore
ISBN 0-7858-0290-8

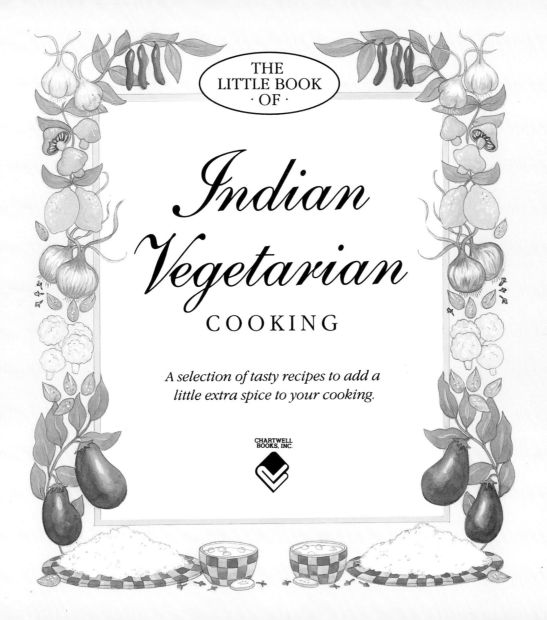

THE LITTLE BOOK · OF ·

Indian Vegetarian

COOKING

A selection of tasty recipes to add a little extra spice to your cooking.

CHARTWELL BOOKS, INC.

Introduction

Indian food is becoming increasingly popular, with some of the exotic ingredients, such as chutneys and garam masala, finding their way onto supermarket shelves. The interest in spices and herbs, and the taste for more international foods, has helped this special cuisine gain acclaim.

The vastness of the Indian subcontinent, together with its great regional diversity, is one of the main factors that give the nation's cuisine its unique standing in the culinary world. The Western fascination with India and its cuisine has developed and matured over the years and at last is gaining popularity here.

There are many parts of India where vegetarianism is a way of life, and vegetarians have been quick to recognize that Indian cuisine offers a vast array of inspiring and exciting dishes. Most people's experience of Indian cuisine, however, has been limited to the dishes offered by restaurants and the chilled cabinet of their local store. Excellent though this food can be, there is much enjoyment to be gained from preparing Indian meals at home.

The spices needed for the curries in this book are among

some of the most easily available and include chili powder, cumin, cilantro, turmeric, cinnamon and cloves, as well as fresh produce such as cilantro leaves, root ginger and green chilies. You may have to hunt further for some, such as fenugreek and cardamom. For these things you may have to seek out an Indian or Oriental store, which is easier in some areas than others, depending on the local population. These stores are a delight to visit with their powerful Oriental smells and bewildering choice of spices, herbs, nuts, flours, dried pulses, and chutneys. They are also an excellent source of unusual vegetables, such as okra.

Indian cooking is not as complicated as some people imagine, and the blending and frying of the spices in these recipes is immensely satisfying. Other people feel they would never adapt to the spiciness involved in eating chilies. Most of these Indian dishes, however, only call for very small amounts of fresh or dried chili, and are not "hot" at all. The recipes in this book are concise and easy to follow, and will inspire and embolden vegetarian and omnivorous cooks alike.

Dhal Soup

SERVES 6

Thick and hearty, this soup can be made with either red or yellow lentils.

PREPARATION: 20 mins
COOKING: 15 mins

1⅔ cups red or yellow lentils
3¾ cups water or broth
4 canned tomatoes, drained and crushed
1 green chili, sliced lengthwise and seeded
2 tbsp plain yogurt or sour cream
1 tbsp butter
1 onion, chopped, or sliced into rings
Salt and pepper
1-2 sprigs fresh cilantro, chopped

1. Wash the lentils in 4-5 changes of water. Drain them well and put them into a large pan with the water or broth.

Step 3 Beat the cooked lentils with a balloon whisk until smooth.

Step 4 Stir in the yogurt or sour cream. Reheat without boiling.

2. Cover the pan and bring to a boil over a moderate heat. Reduce the heat and simmer for about 10-15 minutes, or until the lentils are soft. You may need to add extra water.

3. Using a balloon whisk, beat the lentils until they are smooth.

4. Add the tomatoes and chili and simmer for 2 minutes, then stir in the yogurt or sour cream. Reheat, but do not boil.

5. Melt the butter in a small pan and fry the onion gently, until it is soft, but not colored.

6. Discard the green chili. Pour the soup into serving bowls and sprinkle on the chopped cilantro and the fried onions.

Mushroom Bhaji

SERVES 4

Although mushrooms are not widely used in India, many Indian restaurants have popularized their use in Indian cookery. Mushroom Bhaji is an innovative alternative to the onion variety.

PREPARATION: 15 mins
COOKING: 20 mins

3-4 tbsp vegetable oil
1 onion, finely chopped
2-3 cloves garlic, crushed
½ tsp ground turmeric
½ tsp chili powder
1 tsp ground coriander
1 tsp ground cumin
¾ tsp salt or to taste
1 tbsp tomato paste
2½ cups chopped mushrooms

1. Heat the oil over a medium heat and fry the onion until lightly browned.

2. Lower heat and add the garlic, turmeric, chili powder, coriander and cumin. Stir and fry the spices, adding about 1 tbsp water to prevent them from sticking to the bottom of the pan. As soon as this water dries up, add a little more. Continue doing this until you have fried the spices for about 5 minutes.

3. Add the salt and tomato paste, mix well, and add the mushrooms. Stir until the ingredients are thoroughly mixed.

4. Sprinkle on about 2 tbsp water and cover the pan. Simmer for 10 minutes.

5. The finished dish should have a small amount of sauce, but it should not be runny. If it appears to be a little runny, take the lid off and let the liquid evaporate until the sauce is reasonably thick.

Cauliflower Cutlets

MAKES 10-12 Cutlets

This unusual recipe is an excellent way of using up a cauliflower that is a few days old.

PREPARATION: 35 mins
COOKING: 20 mins

---

1 small cauliflower
2 medium potatoes
2 tbsp vegetable oil plus oil for frying
¼ tsp black mustard seeds
½ tsp cumin seeds
1 large onion, finely chopped
1 fresh green chili, seeded and finely chopped
1 tsp ground fennel
1 tsp ground coriander
¼-½ tsp chili powder or cayenne
½ tsp salt or to taste
½ cup all-purpose flour
2 tbsp chopped cilantro

---

1. Cook the whole cauliflower in boiling water for 6-8 minutes, then drain and cool.

2. Boil the potatoes in their skins, and peel them. Chop the cauliflower coarsely and mash it with the potatoes.

3. Heat the 2 tbsp oil over medium heat and fry mustard seeds until they crackle, then add the cumin seeds.

4. Add the onion and green chili, stir, and fry for 4-5 minutes, or until the onion is soft. Add the spices and salt, stir, and cook over a low heat for 2-3 minutes.

5. Remove the pan from heat and add the potatoes, cauliflower, flour and cilantro. Stir and mix thoroughly.

6. Let the mixture cool completely, then divide it into 10-12 cutlets, each about ⅛-inch thick.

7. Heat the oil over medium heat in a skillet, and fry the cutlets until golden brown on both sides. Drain on paper towel.

Egg & Potato Dum

SERVES 4-6

Hard-boiled curried eggs are very popular in the north-eastern part of India.

PREPARATION: 15 mins
COOKING: 35 mins

---

6 hard-boiled eggs, shelled
5 tbsp vegetable oil
1 lb potatoes, peeled and quartered
Pinch each of chili powder and ground
   turmeric
1 large onion, finely chopped
½-inch fresh ginger root, grated
1 cinnamon stick, broken
2 black cardamom pods, split open at the top
4 whole cloves
1 fresh green chili, chopped
1 small can of tomatoes
½ tsp ground turmeric
2 tsp ground coriander
1 tsp ground fennel seeds
¼-½ tsp chili powder (optional)
1 cup warm water
1 tbsp chopped cilantro

---

1. Make 4 slits lengthwise on each egg, leaving about ½-inch gap at either end.

2. Heat the oil in a nonstick pan. Fry the potatoes for 10 minutes until they are well browned. Remove and keep aside.

3. Take the pan off the heat, and stir in the turmeric and chili mixture. Add the eggs and fry until well browned. Remove and set aside.

4. In the same oil, fry the onion, ginger, cinnamon, cardamom, cloves and green chili for 6-7 minutes, or until the onion is lightly browned.

5. Add half the tomatoes, stir, and fry for 2-3 minutes or until they break up.

6. Add the turmeric, ground coriander, fennel and chili powder (if used); stir and fry for 3-4 minutes. Add the rest of the tomatoes and fry for 4-5 minutes, stirring frequently.

7. Add the potatoes, salt and the water, bring to a boil, cover the pan tightly, and simmer until the potatoes are tender, stirring occasionally.

8. Add the eggs and simmer, uncovered, for 5-6 minutes, stirring once or twice. Stir in the cilantro and remove from heat.

Aloo Gobi

SERVES 3-4

This is a delicious dry vegetable curry.

PREPARATION: 10 mins
COOKING: 10-12 mins

---

1 large onion, chopped
4 tbsp ghee or oil
2 medium potatoes, peeled and cut into chunks
1 medium cauliflower, cut into small florets
2-3 green chilies, chopped
2 sprigs cilantro, chopped
2-inch piece fresh ginger root, peeled and
    finely chopped
Salt to taste
Juice of 1 lemon
2 tsp garam masala

---

1. Fry the onion in the ghee or oil for 2-3 minutes, or until just tender. Add the potatoes and fry for 2-3 minutes.

2. Add the cauliflower, stir and fry for 4-5 minutes. Add the green chilies, cilantro, ginger and salt. Mix well.

3. Cover and cook for 5-6 minutes on a low heat, or until the potatoes are tender.

4. Sprinkle with the lemon juice and garam masala before serving.

Kidney Bean Curry

SERVES 4

The kidney beans are wonderfully enhanced by the flavor of the spices in this delicious curry.

PREPARATION: 20 mins
COOKING: 35 mins

2 tbsp vegetable oil
1 large onion, sliced
2 cloves garlic, crushed
2 green chilies, seeded and chopped
2 tsp grated fresh ginger root
1 tsp chili powder
1 tsp ground coriander
1 tsp ground cumin
1 tsp garam masala
1 cinnamon stick
14-oz can chopped tomatoes
1 bay leaf
2 cups drained, canned red kidney beans
Salt and freshly ground black pepper
Chopped fresh cilantro, to garnish

1. Heat the oil in a large saucepan and fry the onion, garlic and fresh chili for 5 minutes.

2. Stir in the ginger and dry spices, and cook for 1 minute.

3. Add the tomatoes, bay leaf and kidney beans. Season to taste.

4. Cover and simmer gently for 30 minutes, or until the flavors are well blended.

5. Garnish with chopped cilantro.

Black-eyed Pea Curry

SERVES 4

Beans are excellent in curries, as they are healthy and absorb flavors well.

PREPARATION: 10 mins, plus overnight soaking
COOKING: 40 mins

1 cup black-eyed peas, washed and soaked
   overnight in water
1 onion, chopped
3 tbsp ghee or oil
1 bay leaf
1-inch of cinnamon stick
1 tsp ginger paste
1 tsp garlic paste
¼ tsp ground turmeric
1 tsp ground coriander
1 tsp chili powder
4 tomatoes, chopped
Salt to taste
2 green chilies, halved and chopped
2 sprigs cilantro, chopped

1. Boil the drained beans in 2½ cups of water for 20 minutes and let cool.

2. Fry onion in the ghee or oil for 3-4 minutes. Add the bay leaf, cinnamon, ginger and garlic pastes, and fry for 2 minutes.

3. Add the turmeric, ground coriander, chili powder and stir the mixture well.

4. Add the drained, boiled beans and tomatoes. Add salt to taste, the chopped chilies and fresh cilantro.

5. Cover and cook for 10-15 minutes over a gentle heat. The gravy should be thick.

Curried Vegetables

SERVES 6-8

This wholesome vegetable curry includes an interesting combination of unusual vegetables, nuts and spices.

PREPARATION: 30 mins
COOKING: 50 mins

---

2 tbsp peanut oil
1 large onion, chopped
1 green chili, seeded and very finely chopped
1 small piece fresh ginger root, peeled and grated
2 cloves garlic, crushed
½ tsp ground coriander
½ tsp ground cumin
1 tsp ground turmeric
2 potatoes, peeled and diced
1 small cauliflower, washed and cut into florets
1 eggplant, cut into small cubes
14-oz can tomatoes, drained
1 cup sliced okra
1¼ cups vegetable broth
1 cup roasted, salted cashew nuts
4 tbsp shredded coconut
4 tbsp plain yogurt

---

1. Heat the oil in a saucepan and fry the onion, chili, ginger and garlic for 5 minutes, or until beginning to soften.

2. Add the spices and cook for a further minute.

3. Stir in the potatoes and cauliflower and cook for 5 minutes, then stir in the eggplant, tomatoes, okra and broth. Cover and simmer gently for 20 minutes.

4. Add the cashew nuts and coconut and cook, covered, for a further 10-15 minutes, or until all the vegetables are tender and the flavors well blended. Top with plain yogurt and serve.

Zucchini Curry

SERVES 3-4

This zucchini dish makes a good accompaniment to a main-course curry.

PREPARATION: 10 mins
COOKING: 15 mins

1½ tbsp oil
1 tsp cumin seeds
8 oz zucchini, sliced into ¼-inch thick discs
½ tsp chili powder
1 tsp ground coriander
¼ tsp ground turmeric
3-4 fresh or canned tomatoes, chopped
Salt to taste
1 green chili, halved
1 sprig fresh cilantro, chopped

---

1. Heat the oil in a nonstick pan and add the cumin seeds. When they crackle, add the zucchini slices.

2. Stir and sprinkle with the chili, coriander and turmeric.

3. Mix well and add the chopped tomatoes. Sprinkle with salt, the green chili and fresh cilantro.

4. Cover and cook for 10-12 minutes.

Vegetable Niramish

SERVES 4

This highly fragrant curry is ideal to serve as part of a larger Indian meal. Vary the vegetables according to what you have available.

PREPARATION: 20 mins, plus standing
COOKING: 40 mins

1 small eggplant
Salt
3 tbsp vegetable oil
1 onion, sliced
1 green chili, seeded and finely chopped
1 tsp cumin seeds
1 large potato, peeled and cut into chunks
1 cup cauliflower florets
1 small green bell pepper, sliced
2 small carrots, peeled and thickly sliced
1 tsp each, ground coriander, turmeric and chili powder
⅔ cup vegetable broth
1 tsp chopped fresh cilantro
Juice of 1 lime
Chili "flower," to garnish

1. Cut the eggplant into chunks and sprinkle liberally with salt, and let stand for 30 minutes. Rinse well and drain.

Step 1 Cut the eggplant into chunks and sprinkle liberally with salt, stirring the pieces to make sure they are all coated.

2. Heat the oil in a saucepan and fry the onion, green chili and cumin seeds for 2 minutes.

3. Stir in the potato and fry for 3 minutes, add the eggplant, cauliflower, pepper and carrots, and fry for another 3 minutes.

4. Stir in the spices and fry for 1 minute, then add the broth. Cover and simmer gently for 30 minutes until all the vegetables are tender, adding a little more broth if needed.

5. Add the cilantro and lime juice, and simmer for 2 minutes.

6. Serve garnished with a chili "flower."

Spicy Channa Dhal

SERVES 4-6

This is a specialty of the north-eastern region of India. In Assam and Bengal this dhal is invariably served during weddings and other special gatherings. Channa dhal is available from Indian stores, but if it is difficult to get, yellow split peas can be used.

PREPARATION: 10 mins, plus 2 hours soaking
COOKING: 55 mins

1 cup channa dhal or yellow split peas
3 tbsp ghee or clarified butter
1 large onion, finely sliced
2 cinnamon sticks, broken
6 green cardamom pods, split open at the top
2-4 dried red chilies, coarsely chopped
½ tsp ground turmeric
¼-½ tsp chili powder
1¼ tsp salt or to taste
2½ cups warm water
2 bay leaves, crumbled
½ cup shredded coconut
2 ripe tomatoes, skinned and chopped
2 tbsp chopped cilantro

1. Clean and wash the channa dahl or the yellow split peas and soak them for at least 2 hours. Drain well.

2. Melt the ghee or butter over a medium heat and fry the onion, cinnamon, cardamom and red chilies for 6-7 minutes, or until the onion is lightly browned.

3. Add the dhal or peas, turmeric, chili powder and salt. Stir-fry for 2-3 minutes. Reduce the heat to low and fry the dhal for a further 3-4 minutes, stirring frequently.

4. Add the water, bay leaves, coconut and tomatoes. Bring to a boil, cover the pan, and simmer for 35-40 minutes.

5. Stir in the chopped cilantro, remove from the heat, and serve.

Saag Bhaji

SERVES 4-6

Spinach simmered in spices and combined with diced, fried potatoes makes a delicious accompaniment to a main-course dish.

PREPARATION: 30 mins
COOKING: 40 mins

---

6 tbsp vegetable oil
½ tsp black mustard seeds
1 tsp cumin seeds
8-10 fenugreek seeds
1 tbsp curry leaves (optional)
2-3 cloves garlic, crushed
2-4 dried red chilies, chopped
1 lb fresh raw spinach
1 tbsp ghee or clarified butter
1 large potato, peeled and diced
1 large onion, finely sliced
½ tsp ground turmeric
1 tsp ground cumin
½ tsp garam masala
¼-½ tsp chili powder
2-3 ripe tomatoes, skinned and chopped
1 tsp salt or to taste

---

1. Heat 2 tbsps of the oil in a pan and fry mustard seeds until they pop.

2. Add the cumin seeds, fenugreek, curry leaves, garlic and chilies. Allow the garlic to turn slightly brown.

3. Add the spinach, stir, and mix thoroughly. Cover and simmer for 15 minutes, stirring occasionally.

4. Melt the ghee or butter over a medium heat and brown the potato. Remove from heat and set aside.

5. Heat the remaining oil and fry the onion for about 10 minutes or until well browned. Take care not to burn the onion or it will taste bitter.

6. Add the turmeric, cumin, garam masala and chili powder, and stir and fry over a very low heat for 2-3 minutes.

7. Add the spinach, potatoes, tomatoes and salt, cover, and simmer for 10 minutes or until the potatoes are tender, stirring occasionally. Remove from the heat and serve immediately.

Potatoes with Poppy Seeds

SERVES 4-6

This quick and easy, but thoroughly delicious, potato dish comes from Assam. Serve it as a side dish or as a snack – simply gorgeous!

PREPARATION: 10 mins
COOKING: 20 mins

---

5 tbsp vegetable oil
½ tsp onion seeds (optional)
1 tsp cumin seeds
4-6 cloves garlic, crushed
1 tsp freshly ground black pepper
½ tsp ground turmeric
1½ lb potatoes, peeled and diced
1 fresh green chili, finely chopped
6 tbsp white poppy seeds
1 tsp salt or to taste

---

1. Heat the oil in a nonstick or cast-iron pan until smoking. Remove the pan from heat and add the onion seeds (if used) and cumin seeds.

2. As soon as the seeds start crackling, add the garlic and place the pan over a medium heat.

3. Add the black pepper and turmeric, stir briskly, and add the potatoes and the green chili. Fry for 2-3 minutes, stirring constantly.

4. Cover the pan and cook the potatoes over a low heat for 12-15 minutes, or until tender, stirring occasionally.

5. Meanwhile, grind the poppy seeds in a coffee grinder into a coarse mixture. Add to the potatoes and fry over a medium heat for 5-6 minutes, stirring frequently. Stir in the salt and remove from the heat.

Okra with Coconut

SERVES 4

A quick and delicious way to cook okra. Roasted and ground poppy and sesame seeds with coconut coat the okra and add a very special flavor.

PREPARATION: 20 mins
COOKING: 15 mins

---

8 oz okra
2 tbsp sesame seeds
1 tbsp white poppy seeds
1-2 dried red chilies
2 tbsp shredded coconut
1 fresh green chili, coarsely chopped
3 tbsp vegetable oil
½ tsp black mustard seeds
¼ tsp fenugreek seeds
2 cloves garlic, crushed
½ tsp salt or to taste

---

1. Wash the okra, trim off the tops and cut each okra into two pieces.

2. Heat an iron griddle or other heavy-bottomed pan over medium heat, and dry-fry the sesame and poppy seeds until they are lightly browned, stirring constantly. Transfer the seeds to a plate and let cool.

3. Reheat the griddle and dry-fry the coconut until lightly browned, stirring constantly. Transfer to a plate and let cool.

4. Put the sesame and poppy seeds and the dried red chilies in a coffee grinder and switch on; when half ground, add the coconut and the green chili and grind until smooth.

5. Heat the oil over medium heat and add the mustard seeds, and, as soon as the seeds pop, add the fenugreek followed by the garlic. Allow the garlic to brown slightly and add the okra and salt; stir and mix thoroughly. Cover the pan and cook over a very low heat for 10 minutes, stirring occasionally.

6. Stir in the ground ingredients and mix well. Remove from the heat and serve.

Curried Lentils

SERVES 4

A classic curry does take a while to prepare, but is worth the effort. Serve with various vegetable accompaniments.

PREPARATION: 10 mins
COOKING: 55 mins

---

1 cup brown lentils
4 tbsp vegetable oil
1 large onion, finely chopped
1 clove garlic, crushed
1 chili, seeded and finely chopped
1 tsp ground cumin
1 tsp ground coriander
1 tsp ground turmeric
½ tsp ground cinnamon
½ tsp ground nutmeg
2½ cups vegetable broth
½ cup blanched almonds
Salt and freshly ground black pepper
Fresh cilantro, to garnish
1 tbsp shredded coconut

---

1. Rinse the lentils under running water and set aside.

2. Heat the oil in a saucepan and fry the onion, garlic and chili for 3-4 minutes, or until beginning to soften.

3. Stir in the cumin, turmeric, coriander, cinnamon and nutmeg, and fry for 1 minute.

4. Add the lentils and broth, and bring to a boil. Cover and cook for 45 minutes or until lentils are soft and most of the liquid has been absorbed. (If the lentils are soft but there is a lot of liquid remaining, simmer uncovered for a further 10 minutes to evaporate the liquid.)

5. Stir in the almonds. Season to taste. Transfer the lentil curry to a serving dish.

6. Serve garnished with the cilantro and shredded coconut.

Vegetable Pilau

SERVES 4-6

Lightly spiced and fragrant, this traditional Indian rice dish will serve 4 as a lunch or supper on its own or 6 as part of a larger Indian meal.

PREPARATION: 10 mins
COOKING: 20 mins

¼ cup butter or vegetable oil
1 onion, finely sliced
1 cup long-grain rice
1 small piece cinnamon stick
4 cardamom pods, pods removed and seeds crushed
4 cloves
½ tsp ground coriander
¼ tsp ground turmeric
¼ tsp garam masala
1 bay leaf
Salt and freshly ground black pepper
2½ cups vegetable broth or water
½ eggplant, diced
½ cup small cauliflower florets
1 cup finely diced mixed vegetables

---

1. Melt the butter or heat the oil in a large saucepan and fry the onion until beginning to soften.

2. Stir in the rice, spices, bay leaf and seasoning, and fry for 2 minutes, stirring constantly.

3. Add the broth or water, stir well, bring gently to a boil and cook for 5 minutes.

4. Add the eggplant, cauliflower and diced vegetables, and cook for a further 12-15 minutes or until rice is tender and most of the liquid has been absorbed.

5. Leave covered for 5 minutes until the remaining liquid has been absorbed. Stir to separate the grains and serve.

Plain Fried Rice

SERVES 4-6

Plain fried rice is enjoyable with many dishes because the mild taste blends in happily with other flavors. The recipe below is perfect when you want to cook something quick, but a little more special than boiled rice.

PREPARATION: 5 mins, plus ½ hour soaking time
COOKING: 25 mins

1¼ cups basmati rice, washed and soaked in
    cold water for ½ hour
2 tbsp ghee or 3 tbsp vegetable oil
1 tsp fennel seeds
1 tsp salt or to taste
2¼ cups water

---

1. Drain the rice and set aside.

2. Heat the oil or ghee over a medium heat and fry the fennel seeds until they are brown. Add the rice and salt, stir and fry for 4-5 minutes, then lower heat for the last 2-3 minutes of cooking.

3. Add the water and bring to a boil. Cover the pan and simmer for 12 minutes without lifting the lid.

4. When the cooking time is up, remove the pan from the heat and stand, covered, for 5 minutes. Fluff up the rice grains with a metal fork before serving.

Pilau Rice

SERVES 4-6

Pilau is always cooked in pure ghee, but clarified unsalted butter is a good substitute.

PREPARATION: 10 mins, plus 30 mins soaking
COOKING: 40 mins

1¼ cups basmati rice
4 tbsp ghee or clarified butter
1 large onion, finely sliced
2-4 cloves garlic, finely chopped
8 whole cloves
8 green cardamom pods, split open at the top
2 cinnamon sticks, broken
8 whole peppercorns
1 tsp ground turmeric
2½ cups water
1¼ tsp salt or to taste
1 tbsp butter
3 tbsp golden raisins
¼ cup slivered almonds

---

1. Wash the rice and soak in cold water for 30 minutes. Drain well.

2. In a heavy-bottomed saucepan melt the ghee over a medium heat and fry the onion for about 5 minutes, until soft but not brown.

3. Add the garlic, cloves, cardamoms, cinnamon sticks and peppercorns. Stir and fry for 3-4 minutes, or until the onions are golden brown.

4. Add the turmeric, stir and fry for 1-2 minutes. Add the rice and fry over a low heat for a further 2-3 minutes.

5. Add the water and the salt, bring to a boil, cover, and simmer for 15 minutes without lifting the lid.

6. Remove the pan from the heat and keep it undisturbed for a further 10-12 minutes.

7. Melt the butter over a gentle heat and cook the golden raisins for 1 minute, or until they change color and swell up. Remove to a plate and then brown the almonds. Remove to a separate plate.

8. Put the rice into a serving dish and, using a fork, gently mix in the fried raisins and almonds.

Index